DISASTER!
IN THE AIR

Jason Hook

RAINTREE STECK-VAUGHN PUBLISHERS

A Harcourt Company

Austin   New York
www.raintreesteckvaughn.com

Look for the Plane

Look for the plane in boxes like this. Here you will find extra facts, stories, and other interesting information about air disasters.

Published by Raintree Steck-Vaughn Publishers,
an imprint of Steck-Vaughn Company.

Library of Congress Cataloging-in-Publication Data

Designer: Victoria Webb
Editor: Kate Phelps
Picture Research: Lynda Lines

ISBN 0-7398-6315-0

Printed in Taiwan   Bound in United States
1 2 3 4 5 6 7 8 9 0 LB 06 05 04 03 02

Acknowledgments
We wish to thank the following individuals and organizations for their assistance and for supplying material from their collections: Corbis 5 top (Hulton-Deutsch), 5 bottom (Archivo Iconografico), 9 bottom (Hulton-Deutsch), 13 top (Bettmann), 13 bottom (Bettmann), 17 bottom (Roger Ressmeyer), 22 (Bettmann), 23 (Bettmann); MPM Images 29, 31; Katz Pictures 8; NASA back cover bottom right, 15 top; Popperfoto back cover top, 1, 6 (Reuters), 10; Press Association 26, Rex Features front cover, back cover bottom left (Sipa), 1 (Sipa), 2 (Sipa), 3 (Sipa), 14 (Sipa), 16 (Sipa), 18 (Sipa), 19 top (Sipa), 19 bottom (Sipa), 20, 21 top, 21 bottom (Today), 24 (Sipa), 25 top (Huw Evans), 25 bottom (Sipa), 27 (Sipa), 28 (Massimo Sestini); Topham Picturepoint 4, 7 (PressNet), 9 top, 11 top, 12, 15 bottom, 17 top (AP), 30.

▼ A blazing jet somersaults toward the crowd during an air show at Ramstein, Germany, in August 1988.

CONTENTS

▶ *The space shuttle* Challenger *blasts off on January 28, 1986, only 73 seconds before disaster struck.*

TAKING FLIGHT

▲ *Lieutenant Thomas Selfridge and Orville Wright prepare for takeoff, before the crash that killed Selfridge.*

Throughout history, people's attempts to fly have led to disaster. In 1010, an English monk named Eilmer strapped wings to his arms and feet, leaped from the top of Malmesbury Abbey, and broke both his legs. Nearly 900 years later, the German Otto Lilienthal made over 2,000 successful hang-glider flights. But in 1896, disaster struck and Lilienthal crashed to his death.

The first flight in a powered airplane was made by Orville Wright on December 17, 1903. Five years later, Lieutenant Thomas Selfridge flew with Wright. A propeller broke, and he became the first airplane passenger to die in a crash.

Today, flying is one of the safest ways to travel. But bad weather, mechanical failure, terrorism, and human error still lead to accidents. And airplanes have become so big that a disaster can now claim the lives of not one, but hundreds of passengers.

▶ *Otto Lilienthal flying his hang-glider. One of his flights would end in disaster.*

THE FIRST DISASTER

The Ancient Greeks told the story of Daedalus and his son Icarus. They escaped from prison by making wings from wax and feathers and flying out over the sea. But Icarus ignored his father's warning not to fly too close to the Sun. His wings melted and he fell to his death.

▶ *Watched by his father, Icarus tumbles from the sky.*

SUPERSONIC

In 1976, Concorde took to the skies. Flying at twice the speed of sound, it was the fastest way to travel across the Atlantic. For over 20 years, it was also the safest.

On July 25, 2000, an Air France Concorde began its takeoff from Charles de Gaulle Airport, Paris. As the plane roared down the runway, the control tower radioed the pilot, "You have flames behind you!" But the plane was traveling at nearly 200 mph (320 km/h). It was too late to stop.

▼ *The doomed Air France Concorde leaves a trail of fire as it roars into the sky.*

As the Concorde soared into the air, fire spread across one wing. Two engines failed. Losing speed, the massive aircraft rolled slowly over to the left. It crashed through a small hotel and into a cornfield. A witness said the aircraft exploded like "a mini atomic bomb."

An investigation revealed that the Concorde had run over a sharp piece of metal on the runway. A tire had exploded and pierced a fuel tank, and the leaking fuel had caught fire. One hundred passengers, nine crew and four people on the ground were killed.

 Firefighters tackle the blaze where the Concorde crashed through a hotel near the village of Gonesse.

DISASTER IN PARIS

The Concorde disaster was not the first in Paris. On March 3, 1974, a Turkish airliner crashed into Ermenonville Forest, northeast of the city, after a cargo door had burst open. All 346 people on board lost their lives. At the time, it was the worst air disaster in history.

RUNWAYS

The world's worst-ever air disaster happened on the ground. The tragedy took place at Los Rodeos, a little airport in the mountains of Tenerife in the Canary Islands.

In the late afternoon of March 27, 1977, two Boeing 747 jumbo jets prepared to depart from Los Rodeos. The first, a Dutch airliner, taxied the length of the main runway, then turned completely around. The second, an American airliner, had followed the Dutch plane down the runway.

The two planes were now facing head-on. But fog prevented the two pilots from seeing each other. Without permission from the control tower, the Dutch plane began its takeoff. As the American pilot searched for a turnoff, he saw the Dutch plane emerge suddenly from the mist. It was heading straight for him, at full speed.

▲ *Shocked survivors stumble from the crash at Los Rodeos. Both pilots had misunderstood their instructions from the control tower.*

The Dutch plane left the ground briefly. It sliced the top off the American airliner, then slammed back down onto the runway. Both planes burst into flames, and 583 people lost their lives.

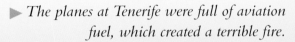
► *The planes at Tenerife were full of aviation fuel, which created a terrible fire.*

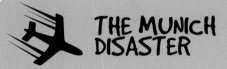

THE MUNICH DISASTER

A runway disaster also devastated the Manchester United football team. Attempting to take off from Munich airport on February 6, 1958, the team's airplane skidded on a runway covered in slush. Twenty-three died in the crash, including eight of Great Britain's best young players.

▼ *Firefighters examine the wreckage at the Munich disaster. The plane crashed on its third attempt to take off.*

AIRSHIPS

As long ago as the 1930s, passengers were making regular flights across the Atlantic. They did not travel in airplanes but in airships. These were enormous, cigar-shaped balloons, driven by propellers.

The most famous of these were German airships called Zeppelins. They provided such safety and luxury that they were known as "flying hotels." The *Hindenburg*, completed in 1936, was the largest Zeppelin ever built. It was three times longer than today's jet airliners and had a dining room with a piano!

▲ As the Hindenburg *exploded, a radio reporter screamed, "It's flashing, flashing, flashing terribly. It's bursting into flames!"*

 ## THE WORLD EXPLODES

The British airship *R101* set off on its maiden flight on October 5, 1930, bound for India. In strong winds, the *R101* started leaking gas. It struck a hill near Beauvais, France, and burst into flames. Forty-eight people were killed. A witness said it felt "as if the whole world had exploded."

The *Hindenburg* made regular flights between Frankfurt, Germany, and Lakehurst, New Jersey. On the evening of May 6, 1937, with 97 people on board, it approached Lakehurst once more. But as the landing ropes were lowered, there was a sudden flash of flame, and the *Hindenburg* burst into a massive fireball.

The airship was filled with hydrogen gas, which burns quickly. Within seconds, all that was left was a frame, like the skeleton of a whale. Thirty-six people died in the blaze, and the disaster brought the age of airship travel to an end.

▲ *The* Hindenburg *sails over Germany. If its flight had not ended in disaster, people might still travel by airship today.*

▼ *The burned wreckage of the* R101. *Incredibly, six people survived the crash.*

MID-AIR COLLISION

On the morning of Friday 16 December 1960, a blazing airliner crashed into the heart of New York City. The United Airlines DC-8 jet sliced through a church steeple, then smashed into the ground.

▲ Firefighters tackled fires in ten buildings after the DC-8 smashed into this street in Brooklyn, New York.

At the same moment, there was a second crash. A TWA Super Constellation airliner broke into pieces and plunged into a nearby airfield.

It soon became clear that the two crashes had a single cause. Among the wreckage of the Constellation, investigators found parts from the DC-8's engines. The two planes had collided in mid-air.

12

Both planes had been heading toward New York airports. But the DC-8 had strayed off course and hurtled into the Constellation. All 128 people on the two planes lost their lives. Amazingly, only six people on New York's streets were killed.

At the time, this was the worst air disaster in history. Strangely, the previous worst had also involved a mid-air collision between the same types of plane from the same two airlines. That disaster took place in 1956 over the Grand Canyon.

▲ *The DC-8's tail somersaulted down the street, and cars exploded as blazing fuel ran beneath them.*

 ## THE EMPIRE STATE

New York had also been the scene of an astonishing air disaster in 1945. In thick fog, an American B-25 bomber weighing 10 tons had flown straight into the Empire State Building. Incredibly, the building showed no sign of collapse and only 14 people were killed.

▶ *Wreckage of a B-25 bomber hangs from a gaping hole in the 78th floor of the Empire State Building.*

▲ Challenger *takes off, blasted into the sky by two giant rockets.*

SPACE

The space shuttle is the world's first reusable spacecraft. It is fired into space on the back of huge rockets, then returns to Earth to land like an airplane on a runway.

On January 28, 1986, the space shuttle *Challenger* was launched from Kennedy Space Center in Florida. For five years, space shuttles had flown without serious accident. But the weather was freezing, and *Challenger* was covered in icicles 60 cm long.

At 11:38 A.M., the shuttle blasted off into the sky on the back of two massive rockets. After 73 seconds, *Challenger* was 9 miles (14 km) high, traveling at 1,900 mph (3000 km/h). Suddenly, there was a huge explosion. The rockets spun away, painting white spirals across the sky. It took three minutes for the crew's cabin to tumble down into the Atlantic. All seven astronauts were killed. Fragments of the shuttle were still falling an hour later.

APOLLO

Challenger was not the first American space disaster. On January 27, 1967, three astronauts died when their Apollo spacecraft burst into flames on the launch pad. In April 1970, an explosion on Apollo 13 nearly left three astronauts stranded in space. But somehow they guided their craft back to Earth.

► *The Challenger's crew, including Christa McAuliffe (left), who had been selected to become the first civilian in space.*

Engineers had warned of the dangers of the cold weather. It had caused rubber seals on the rockets to leak blazing fuel. *Challenger* never should have taken off.

▼ Challenger *explodes. Its rockets were carrying thousands of tons of explosive fuel.*

SHOOT DOWN

On the night of August 31, 1983, a Korean airliner, Flight 007, was flying from Anchorage, Alaska, to Seoul, South Korea. It sent out a radio message at 3:26 A.M., then vanished.

Over the following days, people discovered the terrible truth behind 007's disappearance. It seems that something went wrong with the computers used to navigate the aircraft. Flight 007 drifted farther and farther off course, until it was over the Soviet Union.

 ## THE VINCENNES

On July 3, 1988, the American warship *Vincennes* was fighting with gunboats off the coast of Iran. When radar operators saw an aircraft approaching, they thought they were under attack and launched two missiles. But the plane they shot down was an Iranian airliner carrying 290 people.

▼ *Wreckage of the Iranian Airbus A300, shot down by the* Vincennes, *is recovered from the sea.*

◄Soviet leaders answer questions about Flight 007. It was several days before they admitted their part in the disaster.

At this time, the Soviet Union and the United States were fierce rivals. There was an American spy plane in the area that night, watching Soviet military bases. When Flight 007 appeared on Soviet radar screens, they thought it was also a spy plane. They sent up fighter planes to stop it.

But 007 was an ordinary Boeing 747 with 269 people on board. Its passengers were probably sleeping until missiles from a Soviet fighter slammed into the plane. It took 12 minutes for Flight 007 to plummet into the sea. The Soviet pilot simply radioed his base, "Target is destroyed."

► Demonstrators in California protest the Soviet attack on Flight 007.

AIR SHOWS

Huge crowds flock to see the flying skills of air display teams. But as the acrobatic jets soar between each other at alarming speeds, they are only one mistake away from disaster.

▲ *Three jets collide at Ramstein, as their display goes tragically wrong.*

On August 28, 1988, 300,000 spectators gathered for a show at an American air base at Ramstein, Germany. The final display was a performance by ten jets of the Italian Air Force display team, the Tricolour Arrows.

The display ended with a manoeuvre called "La Bomba." In this, five jets flew between four others, parallel to the spectators but only 200 feet (60 m) above their heads. Meanwhile, a tenth jet raced above them, straight at the crowd.

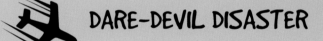
The blazing jet crashes to the ground, and tumbles toward the crowd.

The tenth jet clipped the tails of two others and was sent spiraling downward. The spectators suddenly saw it somersaulting toward them, exploding into flames. Burning debris was scattered over the crowd.

The three pilots and 67 spectators died, and over 300 people suffered serious burns. The pilot of the tenth jet had said before the display, "Human error is always possible."

▼ *The spectators at Ramstein run for their lives. One man said later, "We were caught in a rain of fire."*

DARE-DEVIL DISASTER

People had often complained about American military jets flying too low near the Italian ski resort of Cavalese. On February 3, 1998, a jet flying at only 350 feet (100 m) sliced through the wire of a cable car. Twenty people fell to their deaths. Witnesses said the pilot had been playing a "daredevil" game.

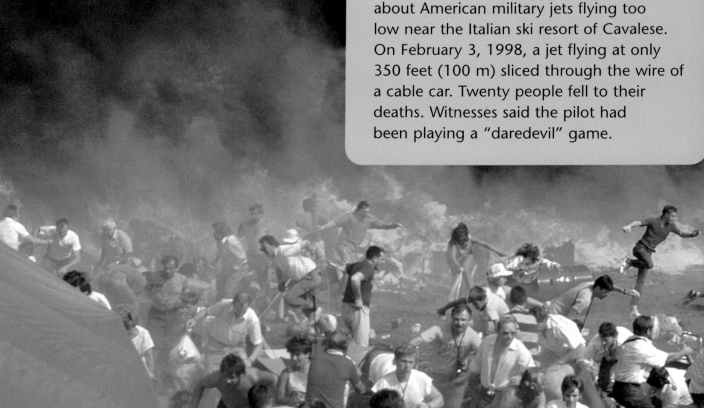

TERRORISM

After nearly a century of flight, people thought nothing of seeing airliners loaded with hundreds of passengers fly over their cities. But on September 11, 2001, everything changed.

On a crystal-clear morning, terrorists armed with knives hijacked four jet airliners as they crossed the United States. The hijackers seized the controls, then deliberately flew the aircraft into buildings on the ground.

In New York, two of the planes were flown into the Twin Towers of the World Trade Center. Standing 1,360 feet (415 m) high and holding 50,000 workers, the famous towers were the tallest buildings in the city.

▲ *The dreadful moment when a hijacked airliner was flown into the Twin Towers. The other tower was already on fire, having been struck by an earlier plane.*

A huge fireball erupted from each tower as the planes struck. Their fuel burst into fires so hot that the steel structure of the towers melted. The Twin Towers collapsed, and nearly 3,000 people lost their lives in a dreadful avalanche of dust, smoke, and rubble.

For the first time in history, every airport in the United States was closed. The skies were suddenly empty. The threat of disaster from the air had become too great.

▲ *After the terrorist attack, a massive column of smoke rose from where the Twin Towers had stood.*

▼ *Devastation at the little Scottish town of Lockerbie.*

LOCKERBIE

On December 21, 1988, a terrorist bomb exploded on an American airliner flying over Lockerbie, Scotland. All 259 people on board, and 11 people in Lockerbie, were killed. At a memorial service, the Reverend James Whyte said, "This was not a natural disaster such as an earthquake. Nor was it the result of human error or carelessness. This, we now know, was an act of human wickedness."

AMAZING SURVIVORS

Today, aircraft travel at incredible speeds and great heights. It is not surprising that air disasters often leave nobody alive. Yet sometimes there are amazing tales of survival.

On October 13, 1972, an airliner crashed into the Andes mountains in South America. Twenty-nine people died in the crash but 16 survived. Stranded without food, they stayed alive by eating the bodies of people killed in the crash.

▼ *Survivors of the 1972 crash in the Andes, who were stranded for ten weeks.*

▲ Firefighters work in the wreckage of the DC-8 in New York. Incredibly, an 11-year-old passenger survived long enough to describe the crash.

When an airliner crashed into New York after a mid-air collision in December 1960, it seemed that nobody could have survived. But 11-year-old Stephen Baltz was found alive in the wreckage.

Stephen lived only until the following day, but was able to describe the crash: "I remember looking out of the plane window at the snow below covering the city. It looked like a picture out of a fairy book.... Then, suddenly, there was an explosion. The plane started to fall and people started to scream. I held on to my seat and then the plane crashed. That's all I remember."

SKY DIVING

On August 24, 1981, a Russian woman, Larissa Sovitskaya, was returning from her honeymoon. The airliner she was on collided with a bomber plane. Clinging to her seat, Sovitskaya fell about 20,000 feet (6,000 m). Trees broke her landing, and she was found alive by rescuers three days later.

SEARCHING FOR CLUES

After an air disaster, a detailed investigation is made. By finding clues that show how an accident happened, investigators can help to make air travel even safer.

 Air crashes on land, like the one involving this Swedish airliner in 1991, leave many more clues for investigators than those at sea.

Recordings of the pilots' confused radio messages during the 1977 Tenerife runway collision led to improvements in the way planes and control towers communicate. After a Russian fighter shot down Korean Flight 007 in 1983, a telephone link was set up between American, Russian, and Japanese air traffic controllers.

BLACK BOX

After an air crash, investigators search for an aircraft's "black box" flight recorders. These record vital information such as the plane's height and speed before the crash and the pilots' conversations. Black boxes can survive massive impacts and temperatures over 1,800 °F (1,000 °C). They are not really black, but bright orange!

Investigators examine the tiniest parts of wreckage. A piece of a bomb's timer was found after the Lockerbie crash in 1988. It helped to bring two terrorists from Libya to trial.

◀ *A survivor is rescued from an airplane that has crashed at sea. Divers will later search for the airplane's "black box" recorder.*

Airlines carry over a billion passengers each year, and they are always trying to improve safety. After the attacks of September 11, 2001, airlines put bulletproof doors in their planes to prevent terrorists from reaching the cockpit. Air disasters are shocking. But it is important to remember that they are also very rare.

◀ *The crashed Concorde near Paris in 2000. Investigators discovered that a burst tire had caused the disaster.*

DISASTER FACTS

BOMB DISASTER

The two airliners that crashed at Tenerife in 1977 were at the airport only because a bomb had exploded at the nearby Las Palmas Airport on the island of Gran Canaria.

RETURN FROM MUNICH

After the Munich Disaster of 1958, a rebuilt Manchester United team won the next match they played. They beat Aston Villa 3–0.

ICE THREAT

In 2000, large chunks of ice falling from airplanes struck houses and gardens 36 times in Great Britain.

TIME BOMB

Nobody knows what caused the *Hindenburg* to explode in 1937. Many people think one of the passengers had carried a time bomb on board. It should have exploded after the passengers got off, but the airship was delayed by storms.

BROKEN WINDOWS

In July 1990, British Airways pilot Captain Tim Lancaster was sucked halfway out of his cabin after two windows broke. The plane was 26,250 feet (8000 m) high and going 370 mph (600 km/h). He was dragged in to safety. His co-pilot landed the plane.

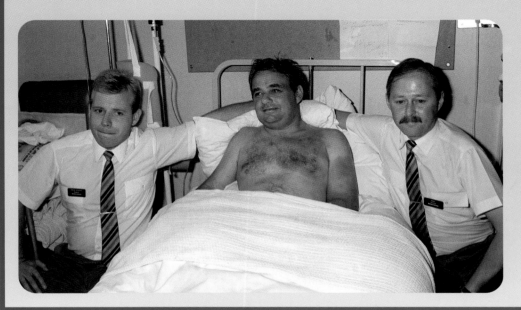

◀ *Captain Tim Lancaster, who was nearly sucked out of his plane when the cabin windows broke. With him are some of the crewmembers who pulled him back into the aircraft.*

SAFETY RECORD

In its first 20 years, Concorde safely carried 3.7 million passengers. Its only accident before the 2000 disaster happened in 1979 and was also caused by a burst tire.

HIJACK HORRORS

The Twin Tower attacks on September 11, 2001, were not the first time hijackers used airplanes as weapons. On Christmas Eve 1994, Algerian terrorists hijacked an Air France Airbus and plotted to crash it into Paris. They were foiled when French commandos stormed the plane at Marseilles airport.

CONCORDSKI CRASH

Concorde was not the first supersonic plane to crash in Paris. A Soviet supersonic jet nicknamed Concordski crashed during the 1973 Paris Air Show.

EVEREST ESCAPE

Sir Edmund Hillary, the climber who conquered Mount Everest, was supposed to have been on the DC-8 that crashed in the mid-air collision over New York in 1960. But he was delayed and missed the flight. He still had the tickets in his pocket at the time of the crash.

▼ *On December 26, 1994, French commandos recapture the hijacked Air France Airbus at Marseilles.*

DISASTER WORDS

Airliner (AIR-lyn-uhr) A large aircraft used to carry passengers.

Apollo (uh-pol-LOH) The name of the American program to send astronauts to the Moon.

Atomic bomb (uh-TOM-ik BOM) An extremely powerful type of bomb.

Boeing 747 (BOW-ing) One of the first and most popular of the jumbo jets.

Cable car (KAY-buhl KAR) A system of cabins on a long wire, used to carry passengers up mountains.

Cargo door (KAR-goh DOR) The door to the part of an airplane where luggage is stored

Control tower (kuhn-TROHL TOU-ur) A tower on the ground at airports, from which air traffic controllers direct aircraft.

DC-8 A type of jet airliner which began flying in 1959. It could carry 116 passengers.

Hang-glider (HANG GLIDE-ur) A type of glider, in which the flyer hangs beneath the wings.

Jet (JET) A plane using a jet engine. Airliners with jet engines can travel faster and farther than those with propellers.

Jumbo jets (JUHM-boh JETS) Large, wide-bodied jets that can carry hundreds of passengers.

Maiden flight (MAYD-uhn FLITE) First flight.

Navigate (NAV-uh-gate) Direct the course of an airplane.

◀ *In February 1998, this cable car was struck by a low-flying American jet.*

Propeller (pruh-PEL-ur) Spinning blades that move some types of aircraft.

Radar (RAY-dar) A system that can be used to locate the position of an aircraft from a distance.

Runway (RUHN-way) The strip of land used by an aircraft to take off and land.

Soviet Union (SOH-vee-it YOON-yuhn) The former Eastern Europe republic that, in 1991, broke up into smaller countries, now known as Russia.

Spy plane (SPYE PLANE) One country's plane that uses electronic equipment to spy on another country.

▲ *A jumbo jet, guided by runway lights. Takeoff and landing are the times of greatest danger.*

Supersonic (soo-pur-SON-ik) Traveling faster than the speed of sound.

Taxied (TAK-seed) Traveled along the ground before or after takeoff.

Terrorism (TER-uh-is-uhm) An act of violence intended to influence governments through terror.

Zeppelin A type of airship created by Count Ferdinand von Zeppelin. Zeppelins first flew in 1900, and they were used to create the first passenger airline in 1909.

DISASTER PROJECTS

NEWSPAPER STORY

Visit your local library and research its archive for a newspaper that was printed on the day after one of the disasters described in this book. Read how the disaster is described. Then, see if you can find more information in books and on the Internet. Are the facts and information the same in the books as in the newspaper? When you have gathered as much information as you can, make your own newspaper page with headlines, photographs, and an account of the disaster.

▼ *Use the Internet to find out about the* Hindenburg *disaster, shown here. Some people think a tiny spark caused the explosion. Others say it was a bomb.*

▲ *A large airport like this one is a perfect place to go plane spotting.*

PLANE SPOTTING

Is there an airport near you? Ask if a parent or teacher will take you to visit the viewing gallery. Try to spot and photograph as many different types of airplane as you can. Which airline uses which colors? Which has the biggest planes? You might be able to find a book from the library that will help you to name the different types of airplane.

AIR DISASTER WEBSITES

If you have access to the Internet, there are hundreds of websites you can check to find out more about aircraft and air disasters.

www.airdisaster.com
This site is packed with information and incredible photographs, covering air disasters from 1950 to the present day.

www.hindenburg.net
This site has lots of photos and information. Watch out for the sound effects!

http://connect.larc.nasa.gov
This website will help you to design your own aircraft.

INDEX

©Belitha Press Ltd. 2003